Stephen - The First Christian Martyr

A Story from Jerusalem

Jim Reimann

Illustrations by Rony Tamir

In the early days of the church, as the numbers began to grow,
The twelve disciples told the others, "There's something that you should know;
For us to wait on tables, while neglecting God's Word, is not good,"
Which was something they, and the other believers, all understood.

5

So seven godly men, full of the Spirit and wisdom, they chose,
To serve one another, and do their chores as they daily arose.
Then they brought the seven to the apostles to bless them with prayer,
Who laid their hands on them, asking for God's blessing, right then and there.

7

A faithful, young believer named Stephen was one of the seven;
He was bold, and was full of God's grace and the power of heaven.
Stephen did many wonders and miracles, which made people glad,
Still, the enemies of the Lord accused him of being quite bad.

The Jewish elders and the teachers of the law became upset,
Accusing innocent Stephen with rumors, and threat after threat.
They warned him of saying Jesus would destroy their holy place,
But noticed as they scolded him, Stephen had an angelic face.

They began to stone him, laying their coats at the feet of young Saul,
A man the Lord Jesus would soon save, and whose name would become Paul.
This young man stood calmly by, as the men stoned poor Stephen to death,
With rocks that hit, crushed, and bruised him, till he took his last earthly breath.

But before Stephen died he preached the gospel of Christ to them all,
Proclaiming God's truth to the leaders, and to the Pharisee, Paul.
Then he lifted his eyes to heaven, as he finished his story,
And saw the blessed Lord Jesus standing, greeting him in glory.

Also in this series:

Jesus is Born! The Bethlehem Story
Jesus is Alive! The Empty Tomb in Jerusalem
John 3:16 Jesus and Nicodemus in Jerusalem
Jesus Loves the Little Children of the World
Saul is Born Again The Conversion of the Apostle Paul
jesus Raises a little girl to life A Miracle in Capernaum
Jesus Heals a Little Boy A Miracle in Capernaum
The Baptism of Jesus A Story from the Jordan River
The Jesus Boat

For ordering information, please contact the publisher:
Intelecty, Ltd.
76 Hagalil
Nofit, Israel 36001
Tel: 97249930922
Fax: 972722830147
Mobile: 972523348598
galit@gestelit.co.il
www.jesusbooks4kids.com